VOL.3

LANSCAPE

GRAYSCALE

COLORING BOOKS FOR BEGINNERS

COLOR TEST PAGE

COLOR TEST PAGE

Wachbergbaude

www.ingramcontent.com/pod-product-compliance
Lightning Source LLC
Chambersburg PA
CBHW080607190526
45169CB00007B/2917
* 9 7 8 1 5 3 7 3 3 2 0 2 4 *